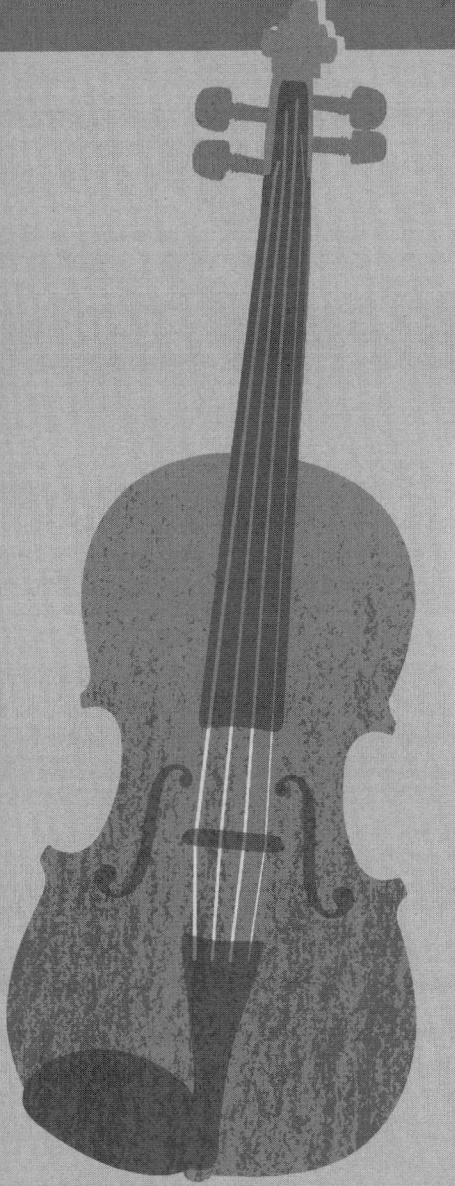

Traditional fiddle music from around the world

VIENNESE FIDDLER

Selected and arranged by
Edward Huws Jones

BOOSEY & HAWKES

Published by Boosey & Hawkes Music Publishers Ltd
Aldwych House
71–91 Aldwych
London
WC2B 4HN

www.boosey.com

© Copyright 2001 by Boosey & Hawkes Music Publishers Ltd
This edition © Copyright 2026 by Boosey & Hawkes Music Publishers Ltd

ISMN 979-0-060-11305-5 | ISBN 978-0-85162-349-8 (complete)
ISMN 979-0-060-11306-2 | ISBN 978-0-85162-350-4 (separately sold violin part)

Printed by Halstan:
Halstan UK, 2–10 Plantation Road, Amersham, Bucks, HP6 6HJ. United Kingdom
Halstan DE, Johannes-Kepler-Straße 5, 55129 Mainz, Germany

All arrangements by Edward Huws Jones
Music setting by Jack Thompson

Cover design by Chloë Alexander Design
Cover image: Guests dance a quadrille on the dance floor at the Vienna Opera Ball,
Vienna, Austria, 12 February 2015: Jens Kalaene/dpa (Alamy)

VIENNESE FIDDLER

Selected and arranged by
Edward Huws Jones

Preface

Viennese music has become almost synonymous with Johann Strauss II and his great waltzes. But of course there were other luminaries: his father Johann Strauss I, his talented brothers Josef and Eduard as well as their colleagues, friends and rivals. This collection includes music by some of these; and apart from waltzes we have polkas (slow and fast), a couple of melodies from operettas and a march. The selection ranges from shorter, eminently playable miniatures to a handful of more extended and challenging arrangements.

The Viennese fiddlers managed to bridge the gap between popular music and the more refined world of the classical composers. Their music has its roots in folk dances like the Austrian ländler and the Bohemian polka, and some of the tunes in this collection have more than a touch of folk fiddle about them. Yet Johann Strauss was also highly regarded by the musical elite of his generation: just think of Brahms, referring to the theme from *The Blue Danube* with the words "not by Brahms, unfortunately"!

The waltz kings were first and foremost *fiddlers*. They led their orchestras from the front, instrument and bow in hand. As a young man Johann Strauss II used to practise his violin in a full-length mirror so he would look every inch the part. They knew how to write for the violin, how to make it sing and dance, and this helps to make the repertoire a perfect foil to the other volumes in this series.

The Viennese composers were working in a commercial world and their public loved novelties and gimmicks. Joseph Strauss's *Fireproof!* is dedicated to a firm of safe-makers and the original score features an anvil. Eduard Strauss's *Clear the Tracks!* celebrates the excitement of the newly-introduced railways. On a gentler note, Johann Strauss I's *Philomel Waltz* evokes the song of the nightingale.

The arrangements in this collection follow the same flexible format as other books in the series and can be performed as solos, duets, or trios, or by larger ensembles. In fact, here are all the resources to recreate a Viennese café orchestra! This music contains all sorts of staccato effects, but a word of warning: staccato does not necessarily mean *off the string*. Often it is more comfortable and effective to play an articulated or detached stroke on the string, without lifting the bow. Some of the arrangements include suggestions as to which sort of stroke to use.

My thanks to my editors, Andrew Hanley and Catherine Duffy; to Anne Dufton and the staff of the Music and Drama Library, Wakefield; to Lizzie Revell of the City of York Performing Arts Service Library; and to Andrea Testa of Quadri's Café Orchestra, St. Mark's Square, Venice, for his inspiration – a Viennese fiddler under warmer skies.

Edward Huws Jones

Préface

On résume souvent la musique viennoise à Johann Strauss II et ses merveilleuses valses, mais il y eut bien sûr d'autres musiciens remarquables : son père Johann Strauss I, ses talentueux frères Josef et Eduard, sans oublier leurs collègues, amis et rivaux. Ce recueil contient certaines de leurs œuvres ; hormis les valses, on y trouve également des polkas (lentes et rapides), quelques mélodies tirées d'opérettes et une marche. Des morceaux très courts et très abordables côtoient quelques arrangements plus longs et plus exigeants.

Les violonistes viennois ont réussi à combler le fossé qui sépare la musique populaire et le monde plus raffiné des compositeurs classiques. Leur musique trouve ses racines dans des danses folkloriques telles que le ländler autrichien et la polka bohémienne. Certains airs de ce recueil sont clairement influencés par les violonistes folkloriques. Cependant, Johann Strauss jouissait aussi de la haute estime de l'élite musicale de sa génération : Brahms par exemple faisait allusion au thème de *An der schönen blauen Donau (Le Beau Danube Bleu)* en ces termes "œuvre non composée par Brahms, malheureusement" !

Les rois de la valse étaient avant toute chose des *violonistes*. Placés devant leurs orchestres, ils les dirigeaient instrument et archet à la main. Jeune homme, Johann Strauss II avait coutume de travailler son violon face à un miroir en pied afin d'être parfait dans ce rôle. Ces virtuoses savaient comment écrire pour le violon, comment le faire chanter et danser, ce qui contribue à faire de ce répertoire une introduction parfaite aux autres volumes de cette série.

Les compositeurs viennois travaillaient dans un environnement commercial et leur public adorait les innovations et les astuces. *Feuerfest ! (Ininflammable !)* de Josef Strauss est dédié à une entreprise de fabrication de coffres-forts et la partition d'origine comporte une partie d'enclume. *Bahn frei ! (Voie libre !)* d'Eduard Strauss célèbre la vive émotion déclenchée par la récente introduction des chemins de fer. Sur une note plus douce, *Philomelen-Waltzer (La Valse de Philomèle)* de Johannn Strauss I évoque le chant du rossignol.

Adoptant le même format flexible que les autres livres de la série, les arrangements de ce recueil peuvent être interprétés en solo, duo, trio ou par des ensembles plus importants. De fait, toutes les ressources permettant de recréer l'orchestre d'un café viennois y sont présentes ! Cette musique contient toutes sortes d'effets staccato, mais attention : staccato ne signifie pas nécessairement *en levant l'archet*. Il est souvent plus aisé et efficace de jouer un coup d'archet articulé ou détaché sur la corde, sans lever l'archet. Certains des arrangements comprennent des suggestions quant au type de coup d'archet à utiliser.

J'adresse mes remerciements à mes rédacteurs, Andrew Hanley et Catherine Duffy ; à Anne Dufton et au personnel de Music and Drama Library de Wakefield ; à Lizzie Revell du City of York Performing Arts Service, ainsi qu'à Andrea Testa du Café Orchestra de Quadri, place St. Marc, à Venise, pour son inspiration – un violoniste viennois sous des cieux plus cléments.

Edward Huws Jones

Vorwort

Für die Musik Wiens ist Johann Strauß der Jüngere mit seinen großartigen Walzern beinahe ein Synonym. Doch selbstverständlich gab es noch weitere große Musiker: seinen Vater Johann Strauß den Älteren, seine ebenfalls sehr talentierten Brüder Josef und Eduard sowie Kollegen, Freunde und Rivalen. Einen Teil dieses Spektrums präsentiert der vorliegende Sammelband, der außer Walzern auch schnelle und langsame Polkas, Operettenmelodien und einen Marsch umfasst. Neben kürzeren, leicht spielbaren Arrangements finden sich auch einige längere und anspruchsvollere Stücke.

Die Wiener Geiger überwanden die Kluft zwischen der populären volkstümlichen Musik und der „kultivierteren" Welt klassischer Komponisten. Die Wurzeln ihrer Musik bilden Volkstänze wie der österreichische Ländler oder die böhmische Polka, und in einigen Stücken dieser Sammlung hört man die volkstümliche Fiedel noch deutlich heraus. Aber Johann Strauß war auch bei der musikalischen Elite seiner Generation hoch angesehen: Man denke nur einmal an Brahms, der das Thema von *An der schönen blauen Donau* mit den Worten „leider nicht von Brahms" kommentierte!

Die Wiener Walzerkönige waren in erster Linie *Geiger*. Sie leiteten ihre Orchester von vorn, Instrument und Bogen immer in den Händen. Als junger Mann übte Johann Strauß der Jüngere auf der Geige oft vor einem großen Spiegel, um sich selbst genauestens zu beobachten. Diese Komponisten wussten, wie man für die Violine schreibt und sein Instrument singen und tanzen lässt – was ihre Musik zugleich zur optimalen Ergänzung für die anderen Ausgaben in unserer Reihe macht.

Die Wiener Komponisten arbeiteten in einer recht kommerziell orientierten Welt, und ihr Publikum liebte besonders Neuheiten und Spezialeffekte. So ist Josef Strauß' Werk *Feuerfest!* einer Tresorfirma gewidmet, was auch den Einsatz des Ambosses in der Originalpartitur erklärt. Eduard Strauß' Werk *Bahn frei!* wiederum feiert die Begeisterung für die damals neue Eisenbahn. Sanftere Töne schlägt dagegen der *Philomelen-Walzer* von Johann Strauß dem Älteren an, der den Gesang der Nachtigall beschwört.

Die Arrangements der vorliegenden Sammlung wurden so flexibel gestaltet wie die anderen Ausgaben dieser Reihe und sie eignen sich sowohl für das Solo-Spiel als auch für Duette, Trios oder größere Ensembles. Hier finden Sie genug Material, um Ihr eigenes Wiener Kaffeehausorchester zu gründen! Diese Musik enthält alle Arten von Stakkato-Effekten. In diesem Zusammenhang eine Anmerkung: Stakkato bedeutet nicht immer „sofort weg von der Saite". Oft ist es wesentlich bequemer und wirkungsvoller, den Strich auf der Saite besonders artikuliert bzw. abgesetzt („détaché") auszuführen, ohne den Bogen abzuheben. Einige Arrangements enthalten Vorschläge für Stricharten.

Mein Dank geht an die Herausgeber Andrew Hanley und Catherine Duffy; an Anne Dufton und die Mitarbeiter der Music and Drama Library in Wakefield; an Lizzie Revell von der City of York Performing Arts Service Library; und an Andrea Testa vom Quadri Kaffeehausorchester (Venedig, Markusplatz) – einen echten Wiener Geiger in wärmeren Gefilden – für seine Inspiration.

Edward Huws Jones

The Beautiful Blue Danube

An der schönen blauen Donau

Johann Strauss II
(1825–1899)

Two Waltzes *from* Gold and Silver
Zwei Walzer aus Gold und Silber

1

Franz Lehar
(1870–1948)

Two Waltzes *from* Gold and Silver
Zwei Walzer aus Gold und Silber

2

Franz Lehar
(1870–1948)

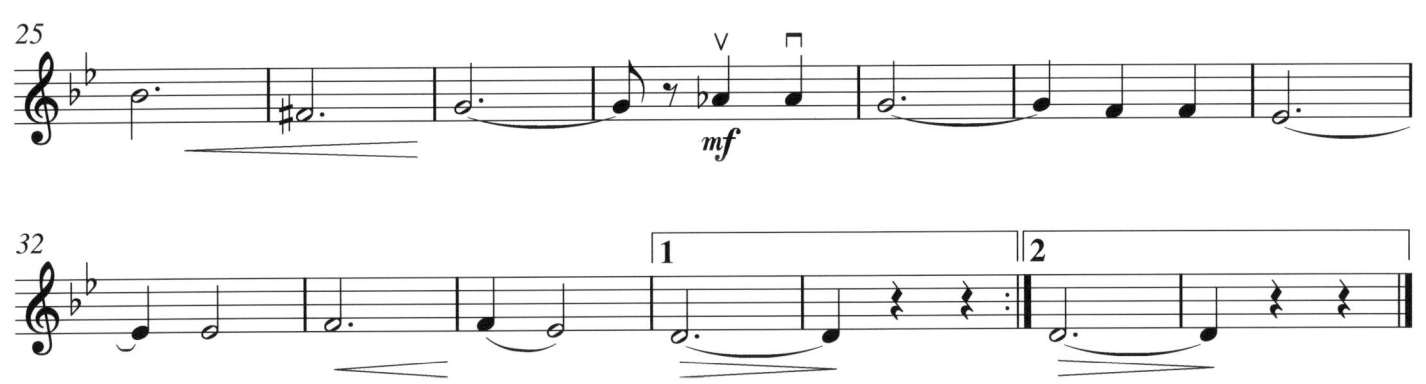

Philomel Waltz

Philomelen-Walzer

Johann Strauss I
(1804–1849)

Russian March
Russischer Marsch

Johann Strauss II
(1825–1899)

Andantino *from* The Gypsy Baron

Andantino aus dem Zigeunerbaron

Johann Strauss II
(1825–1899)

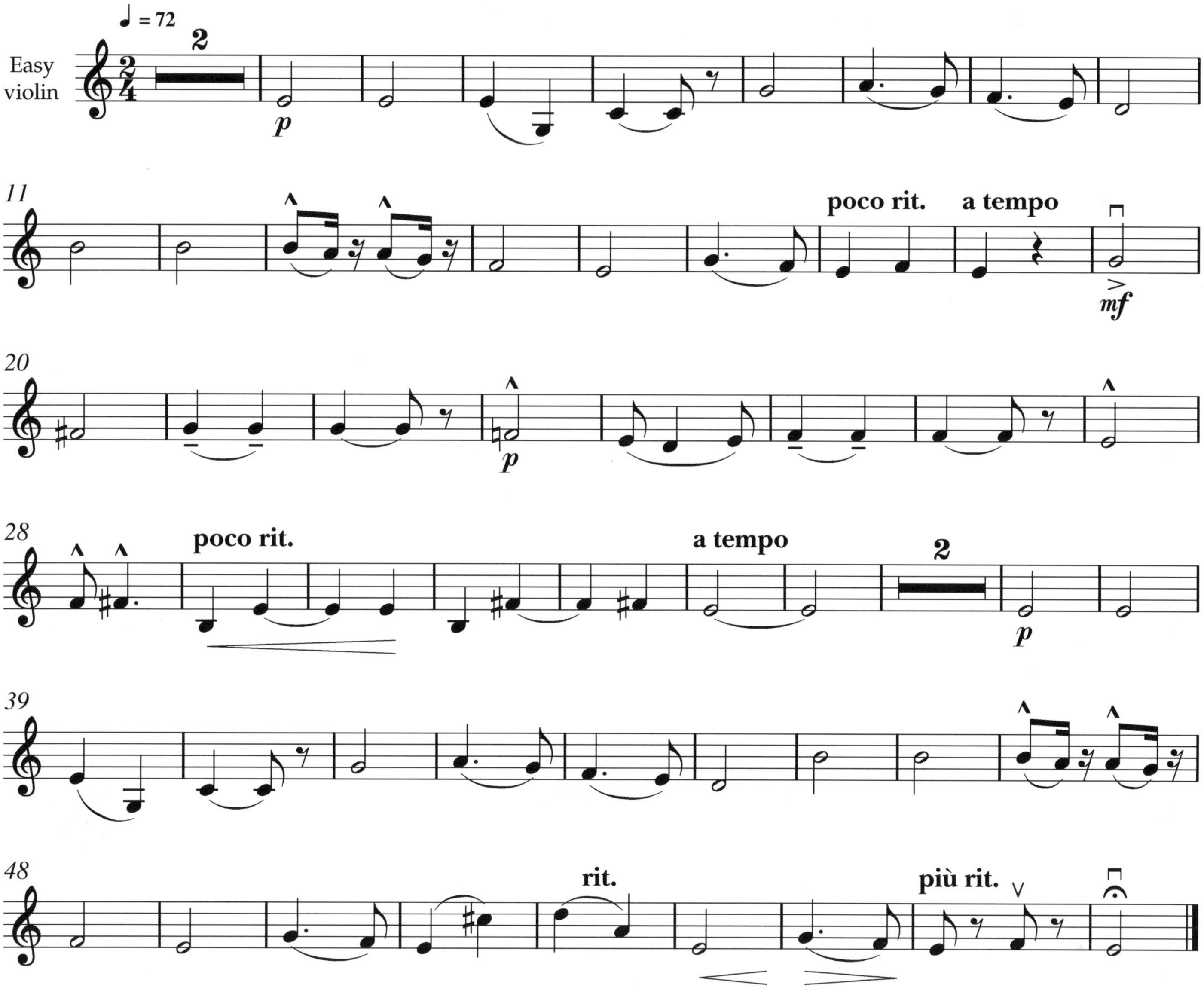
♩ = 72
Easy violin
2
p
11
poco rit.
a tempo
mf
20
p
28
poco rit.
a tempo
2
p
39
48
rit.
più rit.

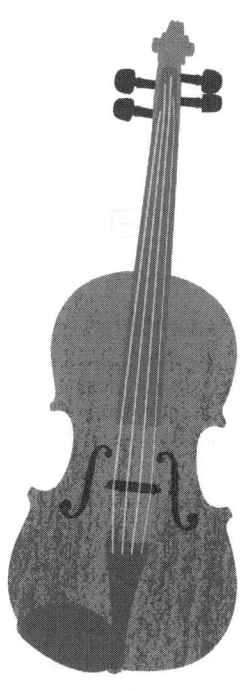

Fireproof!
Feuerfest!

Josef Strauss
(1827–1870)

* Stamp here – see preface. If you have an anvil or a suitable percussion instrument, it could play here and off-beat quavers
throughout fortissimo passages

Polka française (slow polka) ♩ = 80

Easy
violin

* Stamp here – see preface. If you have an anvil or a suitable percussion instrument, it could play here and off-beat quavers
throughout fortissimo passages

The Schönbrunn Palace

Die Schönbrunner

Joseph Lanner
(1801–1843)

The Emperor Waltz
Kaiser-Walzer

Johann Strauss II
(1825–1899)

Roses from the South

Rosen aus dem Süden

Johann Strauss II
(1825–1899)

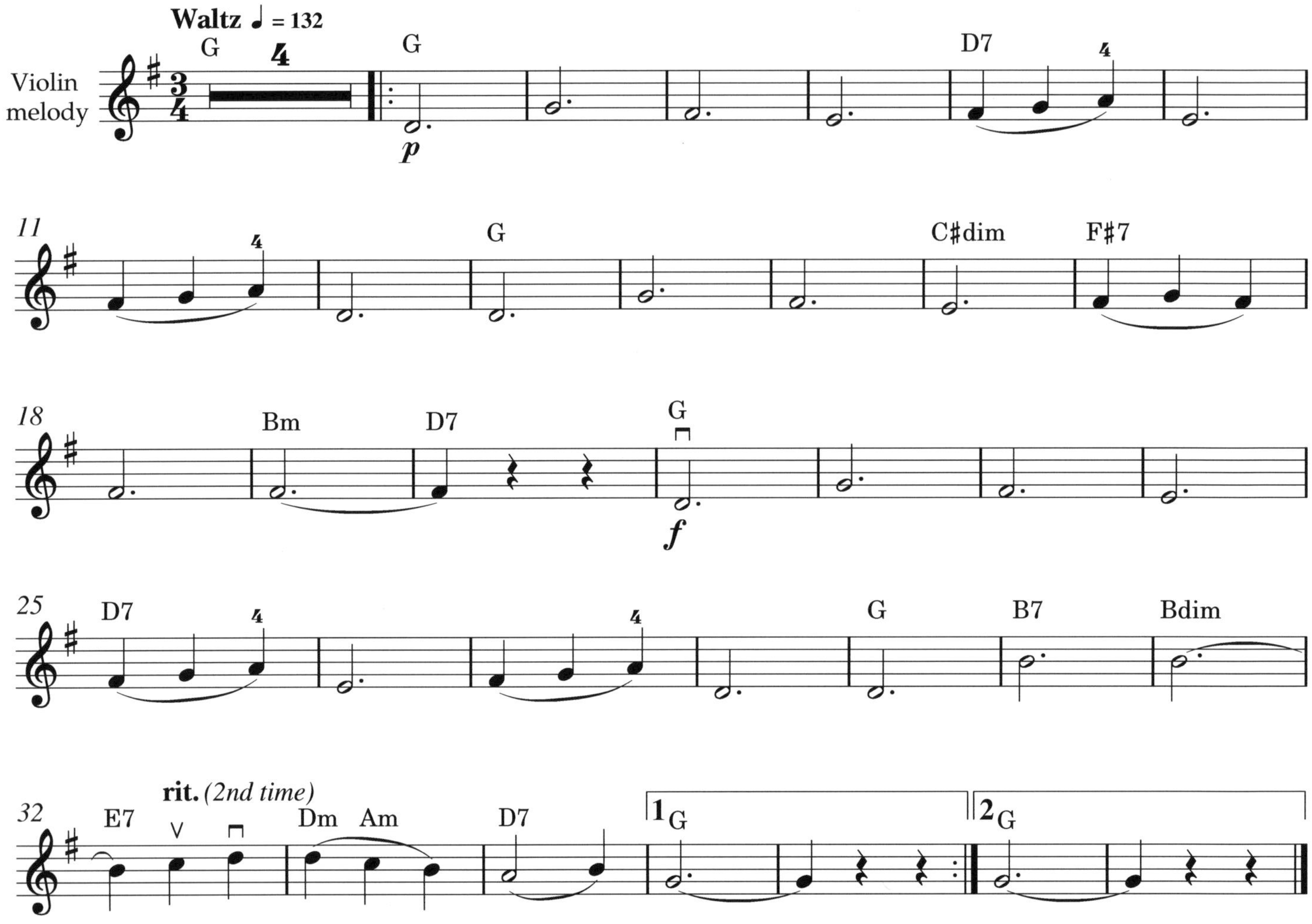

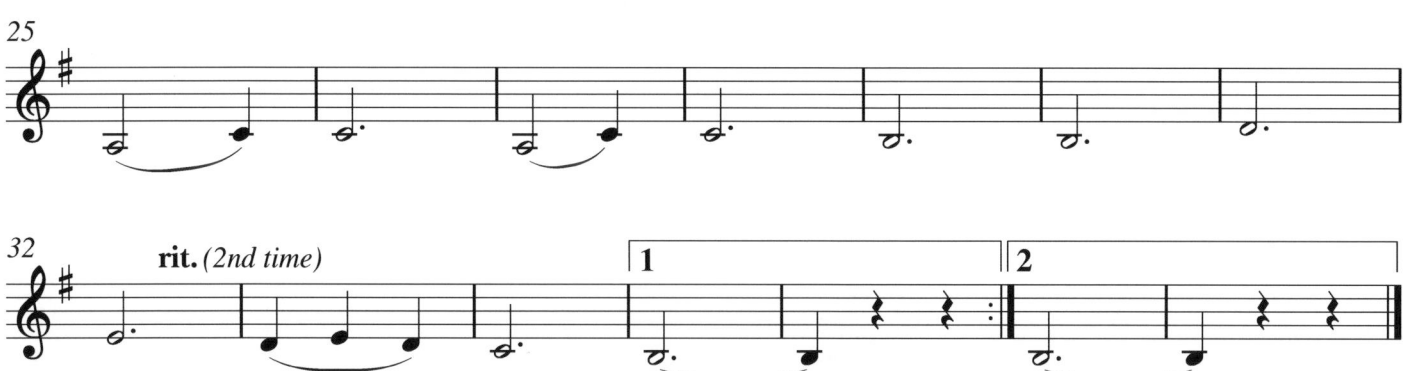

Clear the Tracks!

Bahn frei!

Eduard Strauss
(1835–1916)

Light Cavalry
Leichte Kavallerie

Franz von Suppe
(1819–1895)

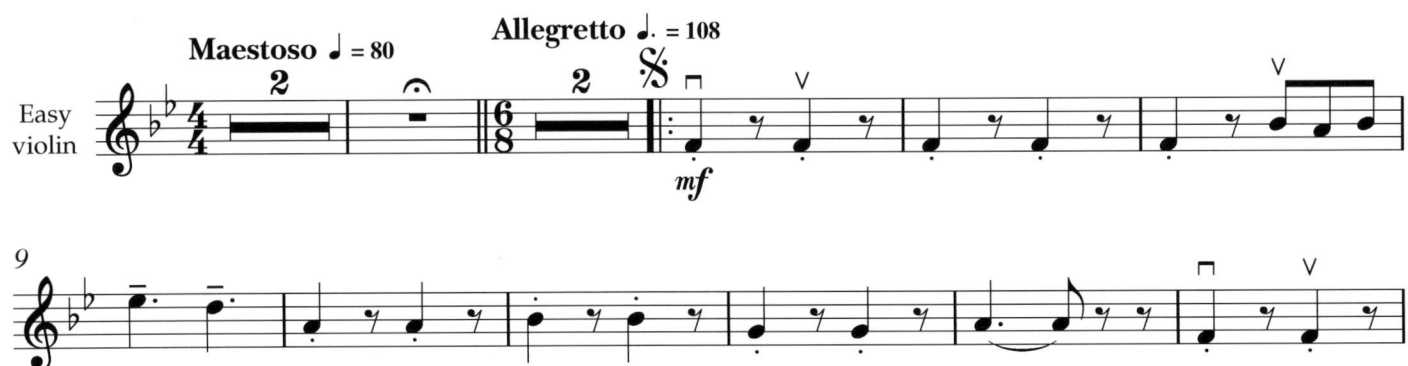

Tales of the Vienna Woods

Geschichten aus dem Wienerwald

Johann Strauss II
(1825–1899)

D. S. al Fine

D. S. al Fine